CRAFTING A KILLER BLURB

WRITING IRRESISTIBLE BACK COVER COPY

A M HADLEY

Spring Street Books

First published by Spring Street Books Ltd 2024

Copyright © 2024 by A M Hadley

ISBN: 978-1-7392903-4-4 (Paperback edition)

ISBN: 978-1-7392903-3-7 (Ebook edition)

Book Cover by ErnieBernie

springstreetbooks.co.uk

FOREWORD

In the vast sea of literature, where countless books vie for attention, a compelling blurb serves as a lighthouse, guiding potential readers to your literary shores. It is the first impression, the handshake that introduces your book to the world, and the key to unlocking the doors of success in the competitive realm of publishing. A well-crafted blurb has the power to transform casual browsers into enthusiastic buyers, converting curious glances into committed readership.

The blurb - or back cover copy - isn't a summary of the story or the contents. Think of it like a trailer for a new TV show or a movie. It needs to persuade you that this book has to be in your life. It's a sales pitch. An advert for your writing. Get the blurb written and a good chunk of your marketing plan just falls into place.

For that reason, you need to do more than sit down with a pen and paper and scribble a jaunty little summary of your book. You need to research your audience and work out where your book will sit in a shop, who will buy it and why. What makes it stand up against or stand out from other books?

It's a couple of hundred words that can take a couple of hundred goes to get right.

For the many writers who've let me blurb them
(and paid me on time)

WHAT THIS BOOK IS ABOUT

When I first started writing, one of the things nobody was willing to explain to me was the 'fine art of blurbing'. For one thing, I had no idea how long those back cover bits needed to be. Nobody would let on about font size, and - like every beginner - I sort of thought I needed to tell most of the story and include lots of intriguing questions - what happens next? That kind of thing.

I now know better.

And you will too if you lash out a couple of quid on the ebook - and probably a few quid more on the paperback, but I hope you'll find my words of 'wisdom' helpful.

I've assumed you know as little as I did back in the day. If I'm patronising you, it's unintentional.

CHAPTER 1

WHAT IS A BLURB?

> **BLURB**: *a short promotional description of a book, usually appearing on the back cover or dust jacket. Its purpose is to entice potential readers by providing a brief, compelling summary of the book's content or story, often accompanied by praise from well-known authors, critics, or publications.*

THE WORD "BLURB" has an interesting origin. Before the early nineteenth century, books came without binding. Blurbs didn't exist. It was coined by American humorist Gelett Burgess in 1907. He used the word "blurb" to describe the promotional text on the dust jacket of his book, "Are You a Bromide?" The dust jacket featured a picture of a young woman named Miss Belinda Blurb, who was depicted as shouting out praise for the book. The name Belinda Blurb and the associated text were intended as a parody of the effusive praise often found on book jackets.

The term "blurb" caught on and has since been widely used in the publishing industry to describe the short, promotional text on book covers.

And any book on the fine art of blurbing wouldn't be worth reading if it didn't mention the almost legendary story of J. D. Salinger who refused to allow anyone to add words to *The Catcher in the Rye*. Simon Prosser is the Publisher of Hamish Hamilton and a publishing director of Penguin Books. Speaking to 'The Guardian' he revealed that Salinger issued strict orders. 'The only copy allowed on the books, back or front, is the author's name and the title. Nothing else at all: no quotes, no cover blurb, no biography. We're not sure why this is.'

~

My assumption when writing this book is that you're going to have a crack at writing your blurb. And why wouldn't you? You're almost certainly not at that stage in your career where you get to lie back on cushions while someone peels grapes and someone else beavers away in a dusty dark corner of your palace, writing blistering copy for the back of your latest book.

If you've ever bought a book, chances are you've scanned the words of some of the best copywriters employed by the publishing industry today. And if the book was written by someone who sells novels and 'How to' guides by the lorry load, they almost surely didn't write their own blurb. Many times, it falls to the editor - the poor soul who just spent a month trying to persuade a reluctant author to change what they insisted is already a flawless masterpiece. Now and then, the author might get involved - they're almost always offered sign-off. But, if the marketing team have decided to go in a certain direction, this sign-off is cursory.

I assume that you're here because you're not at that lovely point in your career where you can rely on other people to do the hard work for you. And even if you could afford it, there are other things to pay out for editing, cover design, and marketing. If you want to produce a book that competes with one from a major publishing house, it isn't as simple as signing up to Amazon's KDP and hitting 'publish'.

And you want to sell books.

∼

One of the greatest challenges in writing a killer blurb lies in the constraint of space. Too many words and nobody is going to read what you have to say. Too few, and they'll miss out on why your book can change their life. There's an art to writing a great blurb. Think of it like hosting a party where every guest needs to know who every other guest is - but they're too busy having a lovely time to listen to long introductions. They need something to hook onto. They want the good stuff. And that's why blurbs exist.

Let's start by cracking open the big 'industry secret': How long should the blurb on the back of my book be?

The average runs somewhere between 150 and 200 words. There is, however, a trend towards ever shorter blurbs, but for now, let's work with the average. The problem I find when working with authors is they want to write more than this. They insist that certain aspects (or subplots) matter just as much as the key story or purpose behind their book or novel. And sure, if you shrink the font or tighten the kerning (space between letters and lines) you could ram a good 500 words onto the back cover, but never do this. It looks self-published, unprofessional, uninformed and tacky. There's an expectation that a professionally produced book features text in a font size between 10 and 12 points, depending on font/genre etc.

And most people stop reading around the 100-word mark anyway.

A tight word count is more than enough to provide a compelling overview of the plot, themes, or key arguments without overwhelming the reader.

You need the blurb to fit comfortably on the back cover while leaving room for other essential elements such as a brief author bio, and maybe a few flashy testimonials. And let's not forget the publisher logo and bar code.

While the content of your blurb is crucial, its presentation is equally important. A well-formatted blurb can catch the eye of potential readers, inviting them to pause and explore further. Use bold or italicised text to highlight key phrases or quotes that encapsulate the essence of your book. Break up your blurb into short, digestible paragraphs that are easy to read and visually appealing.

The visual presentation of your back cover blurb is just as important as its content. Integrating text with your book cover design can significantly affect how potential readers perceive and engage with your book. Here are some key considerations when it comes to the visual elements of your blurb:

The font you choose for your blurb should be legible, visually appealing, and consistent with your book's genre and tone. For example, a serif font may be more suitable for a historical fiction novel, while a modern sans-serif font may work better for a contemporary self-help book. Make sure the font size is large enough to be easily readable, even from a distance or in a thumbnail image online.

The colour scheme of your blurb should complement and enhance your book cover design. Consider using colours that contrast well with the background to ensure the text stands out. If your cover features a dominant colour, you can incorporate that colour into your blurb text or background to create a cohesive visual experience. However, be cautious not to overpower the text with too many colours or busy patterns that may hinder readability.

The placement of your blurb text on the back cover is crucial for both visual appeal and readability. Consider leaving sufficient margins around the text to create a sense of balance and avoid a cluttered appearance. If your book cover features artwork or images, ensure that the blurb text doesn't obscure or compete with these elements. You can also experiment with different text alignments, such as left-aligned, right-aligned, or justified, to find the most visually pleasing and readable layout.

Don't underestimate the power of white space in your blurb design.

White space, or the absence of text or graphics, can help create a sense of balance, clarity, and sophistication. It allows the blurb text to breathe and makes it easier for readers to focus on the content. Avoid cramming too much text onto the back cover, as it can overwhelm readers and discourage them from engaging with your blurb.

So how do you condense the essence of your 60,000-word masterpiece into a mere 200 words or fewer? This is a task that demands precision, creativity, and a deep understanding of your book's core message. Every word must be chosen with care, each sentence crafted to convey the heart and soul of your work. Like a skilled alchemist, you need to distil the gold from the dross, extracting the most compelling elements of your story or your arguments, and presenting them in a single concise, irresistible package.

Any blurb writer worth his or her salt won't simply write a summary of the story or arguments or ideas contained between the covers of a book. They need to present them in a certain way. They need to polish the frame holding the picture. They don't need to lie, but they do need to embroider the truth.

Most times, the back cover blurb is what you'll use to sell your book elsewhere - on Amazon and other online shops. It'll be quoted in reviews and marketing materials such as press releases. Think of it as a letter written to a stranger telling them why they need your book in their lives.

You only need to get it right once. But you do need to get it right.

To create a blurb that resonates with potential readers, you first need to work out just who your audience is. Get the customer right and everything else falls into place.

Who reads books like the one you've written? Where do they live? What do they like to do? What are their interests, desires, and frustrations? What motivates them to pick up a book and lose themselves in its pages?

By delving into the workings of your ideal reader, you'll be able to tailor your blurb so that it speaks directly to their hearts and minds.

Whether you are writing fiction or non-fiction, this blurb should be a mirror that reflects the aspirations, fears, and dreams of your target audience, inviting them to see themselves within the pages of your book.

We'll talk more about ways to find your audience and pick words that get them reading later in this book.

$$\sim$$

A killer blurb is not merely a summary of your book's plot or subject matter; it functions as an emotional hook to grab readers by the heartstrings. It should evoke a visceral response, whether that means excitement, intrigue, fear, or anticipation. By tapping into the power of emotion, you create a connection with potential readers, forging a bond that compels them to explore your words.

A great blurb ignites curiosity, leaving readers with questions that can only be answered by reading what you've got to say. It should hint at the mysteries, conflicts, arguments and revelations within ... but all the time making sure you don't give too much away. Like a skilled magician, this is where you offer a tantalising glimpse of the wonders that lie within while keeping the full extent of your literary magic hidden until the moment is right.

Crafting a killer blurb relies heavily on the power of language. Every word must earn its place and create a vivid, engaging, and persuasive narrative. Use active verbs to convey a sense of urgency and excitement, drawing readers into the heart of your story or the world about which you're writing. Employ sensory details that paint a picture in the reader's mind. Consider the rhythm and flow of your sentences, making sure that each one

builds upon the last, building to a crescendo of anticipation.

But beware. This isn't the time to break all those 'show
don't tell' and 'active writing' rules. Sure, you can indulge
yourself in a little alliteration, help yourself to the odd
metaphor, and unleash repetition to add depth and rich-
ness to your language, making your blurb memorable and
impactful. But if you want your readers to think your book
is hilarious and something they need in their lives, you
need to show this with examples. Get that across in your
writing.

A rule of great stand-up comedy is to keep the set-up to
your punchline short. Try to say no more than five words
to set up the joke. That applies here. For the love of God,
never tell them it's 'hilarious'. That's just another way of
telling the good people of *Good Reads* to take their best
shot.

A good rule to stick with when writing your blurb is to
make sure each sentence you write has no more than one
break (i.e. a comma or a semicolon). This helps you avoid
run-on sentences or information dumps.

And no matter what. You're not standing up in a
university lecture theatre. You're not applying for a job.
Avoid writing your non-fiction blurb to read like a CV.
Avoid turning your fiction blurb into an argument for or
against something.

You're a better writer than that.

~

Crafting a killer blurb is an iterative process that requires
testing and refinement. Share your blurb with beta readers,
fellow authors, and members of your target audience to

gauge their reactions and gather feedback. Pay attention to the words and phrases that resonate with them, as well as any points of confusion or disinterest.

Use this feedback to refine your blurb, honing it until it shines like a polished gem. Remember, a great blurb is not created in a single sitting; it results from careful revision, experimentation, and a willingness to embrace constructive criticism.

In the competitive world of publishing, a killer blurb is your gateway to success. It's the key that unlocks the doors of opportunity, inviting readers to explore whatever literary landscape you have crafted with passion and dedication.

And yes, this is so very different to the creative side of writing in many ways. And yet so alike. But you do need to get your mind into marketing mode. As crude and unwelcome as it may sound to someone who considers themselves an 'artist', now you need to shift product. If it helps, build a new character. A guy who can sell ice to Inuits. How would he talk about your story?

By mastering the art of writing a compelling blurb, you not only increase your chances of generating sales but also establish yourself as a skilled wordsmith, capable of captivating audiences and leaving a lasting impression.

～

As you embark on this journey to create a blurb that sells, remember the power of words to entice, engage, and enchant. Embrace the challenge of distilling the essence of your book into a concise, emotionally charged narrative that speaks directly to the hearts and minds of your target audience. With each carefully chosen word, you build a bridge between your literary world and readers who yearn to explore it.

In the chapters that follow, I'll delve deeper into the secrets of building great blurbs, exploring techniques, case studies, and real-world examples that will equip you with the tools and insights you need to succeed. Whether you are a seasoned author or a newcomer to the world of publishing, this guide will empower you to transform casual browsers into enthusiastic buyers and cultivate a devoted following for your literary works.

CHAPTER 2
THE BASICS

AS AN AUTHOR, you pour your heart and soul into creating a captivating story or a compelling guide that you believe will resonate with readers. However, before a potential reader even has the chance to lose themselves in your words, they encounter the blurb—a concise yet powerful piece of writing that can make or break their decision to pick up your book.

You have limited space to convince the reader that the book they're holding or staring at on a computer screen is worth their time and investment. Your blurb should be engaging, intriguing, and compelling, all while accurately representing the essence of your story or explaining what they'll learn by handing over their credit card details.

To create a blurb that truly captivates readers, it's essential to understand the key components that make it effective.

Let's look at this first in terms of how to write the blurb for a novel - a work of fiction. And these rules matter just as much for children's books as for those aimed at older readers.

FICTION

A killer fiction blurb should include the following elements:

Hook: The opening line of your blurb should immediately grab the reader's attention. It could be a thought-provoking question, a bold statement, or an intriguing scenario that sets the stage for the story to come.

Main Conflict: Every great story revolves around a central conflict or challenge that the protagonist must overcome. Your blurb should hint at this conflict without giving away too much, creating a sense of tension and anticipation that compels the reader to find out more.

Characters: Introduce your main characters (only) in a way that makes them relatable and intriguing. Provide a brief glimpse into their personalities, goals, or struggles, allowing readers to form an emotional connection.

BUT: Don't give away the ending. Please tell me you know that. I'm not going to write a whole chapter explaining why. You can leave out most of the final act of the story, but you still need to hint at the consequences with a big cliffhanger. Just remember, everyone hates a spoiler. End of.

. . .

Stakes: What is at stake for the characters in your story? What will happen if they fail to achieve their goals or overcome any obstacles you've placed in their path? Hinting at the stakes makes the reader feel invested in the outcome of the story. Connect emotionally with the reader by highlighting the universal themes or emotions explored in the book.

Unique Selling Proposition: Clarify what makes this book different or better than others in its category.

Call to Action: Conclude with a strong call to action that encourages the reader to buy or read more.

Tone and Voice: Your blurb should capture the tone and voice of your book, giving readers a sense of the overall mood and style they can expect. Whether your story is dark and suspenseful, light-hearted and humorous, or emotionally gripping, your blurb should reflect this. The opening line of your blurb is crucial in capturing the reader's attention and setting the tone for what's to come. A great hook should be intriguing, provocative, and impossible to ignore.

"In a world where dreams are forbidden, one girl dares rebel."

"A murder. A secret. A race against time to uncover the truth."

"When love and duty collide, which will prevail?"

Notice how each of these hooks draws in the reader, hinting at some sort of central conflict and creating a sense of intrigue.

Craft multiple versions of your hook, experimenting with different angles and approaches until you find one that truly resonates.

Your blurb should introduce only the main characters in a way that makes them memorable and relatable. Focus on their most interesting traits, goals, or challenges, giving readers a reason to care about their journey.

Use strong, descriptive adjectives to capture their essence (e.g., "a determined woman," "a detective haunted by the one that got away," "an unlikely rebel").

Highlight motivations or desires (e.g., "driven by a thirst for revenge," "longing for a place to call home," "making good past mistakes").

Create contrast or conflict (e.g., "she saves lives, he takes them," "forbidden love tearing apart two families").

Remember, your goal is to make readers invested in your characters' lives and eager to follow their story.

Every compelling story revolves around a central conflict or challenge that the protagonist must overcome. Your blurb should hint at this conflict without giving away too much, creating a sense of tension and anticipation. Consider the following examples:

When a mysterious stranger arrives in town, long-buried secrets threaten to unravel the fabric of a tight-knit community.

In a world where magic is forbidden, one girl discovers a power that could change everything—if it doesn't destroy her first.

A chance encounter on a train propels two strangers into a dangerous game of cat and mouse, blurring the lines between truth and deception.

These examples tease a central conflict without

revealing the entire plot. They create a sense of intrigue, leaving readers wondering how the story will unfold and what challenges the characters will face. Talk about no more than two characters by name, use archetypes for the rest (i.e. princess, hero, etc.) and avoid trying to hint at (or worse, detail) any subplots.

The language and structure of your blurb are just as important as the content itself. Every word counts, so choose them carefully to create maximum impact.

- Use active, engaging language that creates a sense of urgency and excitement.
- Vary your sentence structure, using a mix of short, punchy sentences and longer, more descriptive ones.
- Employ powerful verbs that convey action and emotion - words you've been told to avoid in writing your story (e.g., "unravels," "haunts," "propels," "shatters").
- Use vivid imagery and sensory details to transport readers into the world of your story.
- Make sure every single word deserves to be there

Your blurb should be a carefully crafted piece of writing that showcases your skills as a storyteller and leaves readers eager to dive into your book.

NON-FICTION

When it comes to crafting a killer blurb for a non-fiction book, there are some key differences to consider. While the overall goal remains the same—to captivate readers and drive book sales—the approach and elements you focus on may vary.

One of the primary reasons readers pick up a non-fiction book is to gain knowledge, solve or understand a problem, or improve their lives in some way. Your blurb should clearly identify the central problem or challenge that your writing will address and hint at a solution or transformation.

Are you tired of feeling stressed and overwhelmed? Discover the proven strategies to reclaim your time, reduce anxiety, and find inner peace

In a world where distractions are everywhere, learn how to harness the power of focus and unlock your true potential for success and fulfilment.

These blurbs identify a relatable problem and promise a solution that will benefit the reader. By highlighting the problem and solution, you create a sense of urgency and value that compels readers to pick up your book.

When readers choose your book, they want to know that you're qualified to guide them through the subject matter. Your blurb should establish credibility and expertise, giving confidence in your ability to deliver the solutions or insights they seek.

The same rules about voice and tone that I mentioned for fiction, apply with non-fiction back cover copy. If you're *shy but confident* in your writing, the blurb should sound the same. If you come across as big, brash and knowing everything there is to know about your subject - mimic this for potential readers.

Mention any relevant credentials, experience, or achievements that position you as an authority. If you have endorsements from well-known experts or influencers, include a brief quote or testimonial.

Just like with a novel, you don't want to give away each and every secret or idea contained within your book. The blurb should tease the benefits or viewpoints and what takeaways readers might expect. What will they learn? How will their lives be transformed? What practical tools or strategies will they gain?

Uncover the secrets to effective communication, build stronger relationships, and navigate difficult conversations with ease.

Master the art of negotiation, secure better deals, and achieve your goals with the proven techniques taught by a renowned business expert.

For years, the people of this land have waged war on their nearest neighbours. How did this come to be a way of life and what might one day bring peace?

By highlighting the tangible benefits and takeaways,

you give readers a compelling reason to invest time and money in your book.

Just like with fiction blurbs, the language and tone of your non-fiction blurb should be engaging, persuasive, and tailored to your target audience. Use powerful verbs and vivid descriptions to create a sense of excitement and momentum.

Whilst fiction writers have to avoid telling their full story, non-fiction writers should avoid dumping the entire table of contents in their blurb. This is a time and a place to showcase and highlight your expertise and suggest trans-formational benefits. Consider the use of rhetorical questions, bold statements, or thought-provoking quotes to grab attention and elicit an emotional response.

Your blurb should be concise yet impactful, leaving readers eager to dive into the pages of your book.

~

As I've said already, you need to know who you think will read your words. You must identify your target audience, whether writing a novel or a non-fiction book.

Who are your ideal readers? What challenges are they facing? What aspirations or goals do they have?

Consider the language, tone, and examples that will resonate with your specific audience.

Share your blurb with beta readers, colleagues, or members of your target audience to gather feedback and insights. Pay attention to their reactions and questions— what intrigues them? What leaves them wanting to learn more?

Use this feedback to refine your blurb, making it more compelling with each iteration. Don't be afraid to experiment with different hooks, benefit statements, or calls to action until you find the combination that truly resonates with readers.

~

A killer blurb has the power to transform casual browsers into devoted readers, driving book sales and establishing a loyal following for your work. By understanding the key components of a compelling blurb, mastering the language and structure, and tailoring your message to your target audience, you can create a blurb that not only sells your book but also forges a deep connection with readers.

Your blurb is the gateway to your world of words—a tantalising invitation to embark on a journey that will captivate, inspire, and leave a lasting impact. By pouring your heart and soul into crafting a killer blurb, you set the stage for readers to fall in love with your characters, your ideas, your world, and your unique voice as an author.

CHAPTER 3
THE ELEVATOR PITCH

BEFORE DIVING into the intricacies of crafting a compelling back cover blurb, it's essential to understand the concept of the elevator pitch and its significance in the publishing world. Most every writing course you take will fling this hot potato your way.

The term "elevator pitch" originated in the early 20th century when journalists would ride elevators/lifts with busy executives, attempting to secure a story in the brief time it took to reach their desired floor. The concept quickly spread to other industries, particularly sales and marketing, where professionals sought to condense their product's unique value proposition into a concise, persuasive statement.

In the publishing world, the elevator pitch has become an invaluable tool for authors to quickly capture the attention of agents, publishers, and - in your case - potential readers. It's a short, snappy description of your book that sparks curiosity and leaves your audience wanting more.

Every movie, TV show, musical, play or book can be reduced to a pitch:

A chemistry teacher diagnosed with terminal lung cancer teams up with his former student to cook and sell crystal meth in order to provide for his family, his wife, disabled son, and newborn. **Breaking Bad**

Two unlikely Latter-day Saints are chosen to serve their two-year mission together in Uganda. While there, they attempt to convert a small village to The Church of Jesus Christ of Latter-day Saints, where they encounter challenges that test their faith, and their friendship. **The Book of Mormon**

OUR FINAL WARNING. It is the greatest mystery of all because no human being will ever solve it. You Have Been Warned. **The Omen**

In today's fast-paced, information-saturated world, attention spans are shorter than ever. Whether you're pitching your book to an agent at a conference or trying to entice a browsing reader to pick up your novel, you have but a few valuable seconds to make an impression.

A well-crafted elevator pitch distils your book's core concept, theme, and unique selling points into a few compelling sentences. It generates interest and curiosity, leaving your audience eager to learn more. It demonstrates your ability to communicate your book's value clearly and concisely.

Get this right and you're already well on your way to crafting back cover copy that will secure your sales.

Think back to the elements identified in the previous chapter: The hook, the core concept, the stakes, the unique selling point and the target audience.

When combining these elements, aim for a concise pitch that can be delivered in 30 seconds or fewer. Practice your elevator pitch until it feels natural and compelling, and be prepared to adapt it based on your audience and the context of your interaction.

Once you've crafted a winning elevator pitch, you've laid the groundwork for your book's back cover blurb. The key elements of your pitch—the hook, core concept, stakes, unique selling point, and target audience—can be expanded and refined to create a more detailed and persuasive blurb.

Your elevator pitch serves as the core message around which to build a killer blurb, adding relevant details, evocative language, and social proof to create a comprehensive and compelling sales tool for your book.

CHAPTER 4
WHAT ARE WORDS WORTH?

YOU WRITE THEREFORE you already know how important it is to get each word in your book just so. Blurbs often rely on a condensed language of their own. The critic D. J. Taylor explained blurb writing as *a kind of semaphore between author, editor and publisher from which all kinds of extra-curricular inferences can be drawn.*

Blurb writers often employ powerful words and phrases that evoke strong emotions and create a sense of urgency or intrigue. These carefully chosen words make the book stand out and leave a lasting impression on potential readers.

What I didn't realise when first starting out as a writer, is that blurbs have rules about structure. Just as stories call for their components to be arranged in a particular order, blurbs also benefit from a purposeful structure. The shape is determined by what matters most to you (and your reader) and the reveal order you feel works best. What I'm saying is, blurb writing can be a creative process as well as a commercial one.

You might start with a small, specific detail like a character or plot point, then expand to a broader theme or the world in which the story happens. Alternatively, you could begin with the wider context, narrow in on a key detail, and then zoom back out to the big picture.

~

As I mentioned earlier, there has been something of a trend for shorter blurbs. Perhaps occasioned by a world of social media where character limits matter, perhaps caused by the fact we're all getting lazy and want an immediate pay-off. Amazon limits just how much a browser gets to see - especially if you're using a phone - before you have to click 'read more'.

Most people will read a blurb when they're on their feet in a bookshop or an airport, or waiting for a train. Their time is on ration. There's so much more going on around them. So many other books and things that demand attention. If they're at home, browsing on a phone, there's probably a TV in the background, or a dog demanding attention, or kids about to run jammy fingers over your new white sofa.

A 2019 study by the Technical University of Denmark revealed the collective global attention span is narrowing due to the abundance of information coming our way. People make judgments about the quality of a product within the first 90 seconds of their initial interactions. A 2018 study by the University of Bath found that people tend to scan text on screens in a non-linear fashion, focusing on keywords and phrases that stand out. This underscores the importance of using powerful words and compelling language in blurbs to attract readers' attention

The pain in writing a killer blurb comes with the

knowledge they still need to tell a story. Even for non-fiction books. They need a beginning, a middle and an end. They must stand alone as a piece of writing even if their purpose is to make you ache to read another piece of writing.

Every word has to pack a punch. Readers rely on short-hand. They stare at the cover of a book for a few seconds scanning for words that will draw them in to stare a few seconds more. Adjectives such as stunning, horrifying, haunting, fabulously camp, dazzling, stomach-turning. All the -ing words we're told to avoid as writers.

Each brings with it a different expectation. Each helps a reader decide if this book is the one that they want.

A talented blurb writer goes beyond the adjective. They find ways to '*show not tell*' - yes that old chestnut.

Fabulously camp might become: "Nyanja's uncle always wore purple, and lace and entered a room with the loudest of whoops". Stomach-turning: "Every one of us has a heart. It beats better inside our chests, not pecked to pieces by a brace of magpies."

The talent required here is to take a list of words that we want to apply to our work and create ten better ways of saying each. There's no harm in keeping that -ing word in the headline, the 'shout line' or the summary of why someone needs to buy your book.

She was a woman who took joy in pulling the legs off a creature one by one - especially if that creature was a cat.
By turns cruel, by turns misunderstood - why was Maria beloved by everyone in that strange little town that never made it onto maps?

Diane would sit in her window smiling at the boys, undoing the buttons of her shirt as they stared. Then, just as she had them turn around and leave. **Some called her cruel. Others a tease. It all depended on what you thought of the boys?**

Mike liked the sound his kid made when she didn't get her own way. A grunt. A sob. And then, best of all, the crack of a slap around her grizzling face when he caught the brat crying into a pillow, hoping to muffle the sound of tears. **You have to be cruel to be kind in Mike's world.**

Just as there are words you can build on, there are words that get 'done to death' and I'd truly suggest you do your damnedest to avoid. I'm talking about words like gripping, unputdownable, riveting, explosive, unforgettable, very readable, provocative and that old fave, groundbreaking. Chances are, even if your book is the best thing ever, it's none of the above.

~

Effective blurb writers often use sensory language to create vivid mental images and engage readers' senses. By using descriptive words that evoke sight, sound, touch, taste, or smell, writers can transport potential readers into the world of the book and make the experience more immersive.

Her mournful song carried on each morning breeze. The lady with the lollipop shoes, ruthless, devious and seductive. The loud, annoying buzz of the blue bottle fly. The ping from your phone. You're overdrawn again. Thanks to the plumber who charged twice what he promised he might.

To pique curiosity and leave readers wanting more, blurb writers often employ cliffhangers or open-ended questions. These create a sense of intrigue and encourage us to dive into the book to find the answers.

An exotic stranger blows in on the changing wind and opens a chocolate boutique directly opposite the church. Friends tell her Tallulah was last seen heading to a party at a house in the woods nearby called Dark Place. Is Don Tillman ready to become the man he always dreamed of being?

By leaving readers with unanswered questions or hinting at unexpected twists, blurb writers tap into the human desire for resolution and encourage readers to pick up the book to satisfy their curiosity.

The language choices play a crucial role in persuading potential readers to pick up a book. By employing powerful words, sensory language, cliffhangers, and open-ended questions, you can create an irresistible appeal that compels readers to explore the pages within.

~

If you want to offend half the world, try describing your female characters as bubbly, feisty, bossy or shrewish (I could go on). Keep in mind more women than men buy books, so watch your mouth. If you wouldn't say it about a man, don't say it about a woman. Even if it's meant to be ironic. The phrase 'strong woman' is probably meant to be life-affirming. But would 'Bob' who gets looked over for a promotion be secretly a 'strong man' despite everything? Probably not. Determined, yes. Find the right words and make sure you're not offending anyone.

Book covers on the whole do tend to reflect and feed sexist tropes. For a while, pink covers were essential for anything termed 'chick lit'. These days, women spend a lot of time on beaches, near rivers, watching something happen in the distance or pulling a 'why me' face.

A 2018 study titled "Judging Books by Their Covers - Analysing the Representation of Female Protagonists on Young Adult Book Covers" by Kimberley Tolson examined the portrayal of female characters on YA book covers. While not specifically about blurbs, it found that female protagonists were more likely to be portrayed as passive and objectified compared to their male counterparts.

Author Maureen Johnson conducted an informal "coverflip" experiment in 2013, where she challenged Twitter users to reimagine book covers with the author's gender-flipped. The results highlighted the stark differences in how books by male and female authors were marketed, with gendered stereotypes prevalent in cover design and blurb language.

A 2019 article by Jo Piazza for The Washington Post titled "The subtle sexism of your open-plan office" mentioned a study that found "women are far more likely than men to be described in novels as beautiful, as having body parts and using their faces to express emotions."

∽

So much for the words. What about punctuation? You may well ask! Because …

Exclamation marks get a bad rap with most writers. Elmore Leonard reckoned that 'you are allowed no more than two or three per 100,000 words'. But some writers love them. Some use them to great effect. In a blurb, they have their place. But remember, blurbs are short. Overusing exclamation marks can make your blurb feel overly enthusiastic or amateurish. More than a couple and it risks coming over as less than serious, too shouty, just too much!!

The question mark seems to be a given when it comes to back-cover copy. Most books seek to ask and answer questions, it seems. Questions create a sense of intrigue and engage readers by directly addressing their curiosity. That said, I'm not a huge fan of ending the blurb on a question - it sort of screams amateur hour.

"Will life ever be the same for John and Edward?"

The thing is, the reader already knows it probably won't be.

"Can they overcome their differences and find love?"

Yeah, they more than likely will

Ending on a question is lazy writing. Easy to do, and it sounds great the first time you think it up, but do you want cheap and cheerful? And cheesy?

Now, what about those three dots? The ellipses.

You'd be surprised just how much hate there is out there for them. I'll be the first to admit they're often used when the author should know to use an em-dash.

An em-dash indicates an abrupt stop or interruption, an emphatic pause, or a break in thought. Em dashes can introduce a surprising twist, a list of elements, or an intriguing clause. Be mindful not to overuse them, as they can disrupt the flow of your blurb.

An ellipsis signals a brief pause, a wavering, or an omission. It might also convey a trailing thought at the end of a sentence. They are pretty much invaluable when writing killer blurbs to create intrigue, curiosity, and a sense of the ridiculous. Just be careful not to overuse them - things get choppy fast.

Keep your punctuation straightforward. Avoid using overly complex or unconventional punctuation, as it can distract from your message. Use it to create a sense of rhythm and pacing. Vary your sentence lengths and structures.

And while we're talking technicalities. Typos in your blurb will kill sales. Find an editor to read it through - if you're paying someone to edit your book, add in the blurb and don't be afraid to ask them if they think it hits the mark. They'll have likely just spent two weeks with your writing, they'll pull no punches.

Remember, the goal of your blurb is to capture attention, evoke emotion, and persuade readers to pick up your book. Use punctuation strategically to enhance your message and create a compelling reading experience.

Mastering all of these language techniques is an art form that requires a deep understanding of human psychology and the ability to craft concise, impactful messages. When done effectively, a well-written blurb can be the gateway to a captivating reading experience and a powerful tool for driving book sales.

And above all else, you need to understand your audience. You need to know who will be most likely to buy your book.

CHAPTER 5
KNOW YOUR AUDIENCE

ANYONE WHO HAS EVER WORKED in marketing will have been told *'know your customer and the rest just falls into place'*. Often by a smug marketing director who thinks they're the first person to ever say this. They might even brag about how this is 'their mantra'.

It isn't.

It's just how all selling works.

Sort of.

And even if you're a writer of fabulously lofty literary fiction who would never soil their hands with the filthy business of flogging books, if you want to make a living from your words and write another book, you're going to have to hold your nose and read this chapter.

You're selling something. You need buyers. And yes, your buyers are readers, but still this is show business, ladies and gentlemen. And you're dancing on the stage for money.

Writing a 60,000-word book requires a very different skill set to writing 150. Especially if the two are connected.

If the 150 needs to persuade someone else to read the 60,000.

This is why it matters so much that the person creating the blurb understands who the audience is for the book. They need to speak the right language and put out in all the right ways.

As an author, it can be incredibly hard to get your head around who you're writing for. Is it for you? Is it for people like you? Is it for people who buy books like the one you think you might be writing? Is it for your Nan?

The biggest issue often comes when you realise you're too close to what you've spent months or years writing to step back and think in terms of the reader. You've written the perfect book that everyone might like to read - regardless of age, gender, education level, or nationality.

It's why copywriters might be better placed to help with your blurb. And if you can't afford them, ask a friend or a writing buddy: What did you get from my book? Who do you reckon will read it?

Some of us authors take to blurb writing like ducks to water. A lot of us don't. We refuse to sanction the removal of a subplot or a minor character. We howl when our 'inciting incident' is revealed.

"But that doesn't happen until chapter five," we insist.

Think about when you go see a movie. Often you know who's in the cast and what it's about. You sort of know what's going to happen and that the joy will come from seeing how this resolves itself.

A man comes home to find his wife has left after what he thought was a happy marriage. Except she hasn't left. She was taken against her will. Something this man will come to realise when he starts to call around his friends.

A novelist will need to spend at least one chapter

world-building. Creating a humdrum everyday, happy life. They'll need to draw the characters and bring the man home. They'll need to describe his shock, and his betrayal and depict how he calls around friends - and which friends and why. How can they put all this in the shop window? They might as well just start at Chapter Six.

Knowing where something might be going often helps the reader find their way into a story - especially when confronted by a new world, a new writer with their own style and new characters. By the time things turn upside down, they're hooked. This is another great function of the blurb.

~

A well-crafted blurb speaks directly to the readers who are most likely to appreciate and invest in your work. They haven't spent any time with your characters or lived in your imagined (or real) world. They need the blurb to convey an expectation of what will happen when they read on. Or what new thing they'll be able to do after they read your book.

Every book has a specific audience, whether it's a particular age group, gender, or readers with specific interests. Tailoring your cover copy to resonate with this target audience is key to selling copies of your book.

So, how do you work out just who you're writing for? Let's start simple. Be honest with yourself …

- What age group is your book best suited for? - it won't be for all ages
- Is your book targeted towards a specific gender or is it gender-neutral?

- What are the primary interests, hobbies, or challenges of your ideal reader? - try not to say reading.
- Are there any specific demographics (e.g., location, education level, occupation) that your book appeals to?

Answering these questions will help you create something marketing people call 'a reader persona'. This is just jargon for a description of your ideal reader. To gain a deeper understanding of your target audience calls for a little more research.

- Think again about books a little like yours. Writers whose books might end up on the same shelf or part of the shelf in a bookstore as the novel or self-help guide you created. Make a list.
- Read the blurbs - what words crop up all the time? What style do these blurbs use? Short sharp sentences. Do they promise something? Do they tug at heartstrings? Do they aim to make you laugh, cry or worry?
- Go online and analyse reader reviews and feedback on these books. Pay attention to what readers appreciate, criticise, and appear to have been looking for when they bought the book - if they give it one star, why? What was missing? And most crucially if the review is angry, why? What promises were broken by a bad blurb?
- If you have nerves of steel and time to throw away, engage with your target audience on social media platforms, forums, and online communities. Observe their conversations, interests, and the language they use.
- Make a list of words that keep coming up - keywords that will help you create copy that when posted on bookselling websites will feed into search engines and send casual surfers your way.

Once you clearly understand your target audience, use that knowledge to inform every aspect of your blurb:

- Use language and tone that you've seen used by 'competing' writers. Adopt a voice that speaks directly to your readers and proves that it understands what lights their fire. Prove you get what they love, and that you understand their interests, challenges, and desires.
- Highlight aspects of your book that are most relevant and appealing to your identified audience. Emphasise the unique value your book offers them. Or if you're giving them something just like they get from a much-loved author (but with a twist) say this.
- Use compelling hooks and questions that pique curiosity and make them eager to dive into your book.
- Include some of those relevant keywords and phrases that you've gathered and that your target audience is likely to search for.

~

In today's digital age, authors have access to a wealth of tools and techniques that can help them gather concrete data about their potential readers. Here are some ways to leverage modern technology and research methods to gain insights into your audience.

Social media platforms like Facebook, Twitter, and Instagram offer built-in analytics tools that provide valuable information about your followers. These tools can help you understand demographics such as age, gender, location, and interests. By analysing this data, you can tailor your blurb to resonate with your target audience. For example, if your analytics show that a significant portion of your followers are young adults interested in fantasy novels, you can emphasise the fantastical elements and fast-paced adventure in your blurb.

Conducting surveys is an effective way to gather direct feedback from potential readers. Using online survey tools like Google Forms or Survey Monkey, you can create targeted questionnaires to learn more about your audience's preferences, reading habits, and expectations. Ask questions about their favourite genres, authors, and what they look for in a book. You can distribute these surveys through your email list, social media channels, or reader communities. The insights gained from surveys can help you craft a blurb that speaks directly to your readers' interests.

Engaging in one-on-one interviews with a diverse group of readers can provide deep, qualitative insights into their perspectives and desires. Reach out to book bloggers, reviewers, or avid readers in your genre and request interviews. During these conversations, ask open-ended questions about what draws them to certain books, what makes a blurb compelling to them, and what elements they look for in a story. These interviews can uncover valuable insights that may not be apparent through quantitative data alone.

Analysing reviews of books similar to yours on Amazon can offer a goldmine of information about reader preferences. Look for patterns in the reviews, such as what readers praised or criticised about the book's content, pacing, or characters. Pay attention to the language readers use to describe their experiences and incorporate those insights into your blurb. For instance, if many reviewers mention the importance of a strong female lead, highlight your protagonist's strength and agency in your blurb.

Knowing your audience is the foundation of writing effective book blurbs. By understanding your target readers' preferences, challenges, and aspirations, you can craft a blurb that speaks directly to them, showcases your book's unique value, and compels them to pick it up and start reading.

CHAPTER 6

STAY IN YOUR LANE

THERE ARE rules (not strict ones, but I should tell you now) that govern the blurbs you write for different genres of fiction. Now that you've worked out your audience, let's think about how to best tempt them into parting with their hard-earned money.

Each genre comes with its own set of expectations, tropes, and conventions. As an author or publisher, understanding these nuances is crucial when crafting a compelling blurb that connects with your target audience.

Mystery and crime fiction readers crave suspense, intrigue, and a puzzle to solve. You need to focus on what sets your murder apart from all the others taking place in books on the same shelf. Is it an unusual crime scene, a twisted motive, or a detective with a distinctive quirk? Introduce your protagonist, whether it's a world-weary detective or an amateur sleuth, and hint at their stakes or challenges. Convey the mood and atmosphere of your story's world. Are we talking about a gritty urban landscape or a quaint countryside village with dark secrets lurking beneath the surface?

> *In the tranquil town of Wellingham, a killer lies in wait for seemingly random victims. Detective Georgina Anderson, still haunted by the one who got away, has made it her job to unravel the threads that bind these murders together. If it's the last thing she does, before retiring to life in the Spanish sun. As she digs deeper, the truth dawns. And it's closer to home than she ever imagined.*

Romance readers seek the emotional journey of falling in love, with all its joys, challenges, and heartaches. Highlight the barrier that keeps your characters apart, whether a misunderstanding, a social divide, or a personal fear to overcome. Convey undeniable chemistry between your protagonists, hinting at what simmers beneath. Hint hard that love may well triumph, leading the reader to settle in for a satisfying and heart-warming resolution. The rule with romance is 'happy ever after' or 'happy for now'.

> *City lawyer Amelia Leonard vowed she was done with men. She'd been let down once too often. Not least by her late father, who died in flagrante with a member of his kitchen staff at the family pile. As an only child, Amelia returns to Stourton to settle his estate, never once thinking her school crush might still be around. And tending the stables. As old feelings resurface, Amelia must choose between the love she left behind and the life she built. Can she follow her heart and discover where she belongs?*

Science fiction and fantasy readers crave immersive worlds, mind-bending concepts, and epic adventures. Introduce the elements that define your story's universe, its advanced technology, magic systems, or fantastical creatures. Hint at the protagonist's epic quest or mission, and the challenges along the way. Convey the scale and importance of the conflict, whether it's the fate of a galaxy or the survival of a kingdom.

In a distant galaxy, Zara, a wandering warrior, discovers an ancient stone that holds the key to all-encompassing power. As she embarks on a journey to unlock its secrets, she must navigate alien landscapes, forge unlikely alliances, and confront a malevolent force that threatens the very fabric of the universe.

Horror readers seek the thrill of being scared, the exploration of the unknown, and the confrontation with the darkest aspects of human nature. Introduce the main threat or antagonist, whether it's a supernatural entity, a twisted killer, or a psychological menace. Highlight the main character's weaknesses or past traumas that make them particularly susceptible to the horror they face. Convey the mounting sense of terror and the seeming impossibility of escape or triumph over evil.

When Sarah and her family move into a secluded farm-house, she hopes to leave her troubled past behind. But as strange occurrences escalate and her children begin to exhibit disturbing behaviour, Sarah realises that an ancient evil has awakened, one that feeds on her deepest fears. Trapped and desperate, Sarah must confront the malevolent presence before it consumes her family and her sanity.

Comedy readers crave laughter, wit, and a light-hearted escape from the stresses of daily life. Open with a clever, funny, or ironic statement that sets the tone for the story and grabs the reader's attention. Introduce your protagonist(s) and their eccentric personalities, amusing flaws, or comical predicaments. Hint at the hilarious situations, witty dialogue, and overall entertaining journey that awaits the reader.

Unlucky-in-love Lisa Doyle is about to turn forty and has had enough of being the girl most likely to die alone, eaten by feral cats. But when her childhood BFF asks her to be maid of honour, Lisa's world implodes as she discovers the bride's new bestie is none other than former school bully, Ginny. Desperate to save face, Lisa invents an astronaut husband, roping in her recently divorced boss, Brian. As Ginny takes charge of the wedding plans and Lisa's disastrous office party video goes viral, she must decide whether to stand up to her nemesis or run for the hills.

Literary fiction readers seek profound insights into the human experience, complex characters, and evocative prose. Highlight the central themes or philosophical questions your story explores, such as love, loss, identity, or the search for meaning. Introduce your protagonist(s) and the internal conflicts or transformative journeys they will undergo. Convey the emotional impact of your story and the potential for readers to connect with the characters' experiences on a deep, personal level.

In the aftermath of a devastating loss, estranged siblings Olivia and Nathan reunite in their home town, where long-buried secrets and unresolved tensions threaten to surface. As they navigate the ruins of their family history and their fractured relationship, Olivia and Nathan must confront the ghosts of their past to forge a path towards forgiveness and redemption.

Crafting the perfect blurb requires a deep understanding of your genre's conventions and your target audience's expectations. By focusing on the key elements that define each genre and using evocative language to convey the essence of your story, you can create a blurb that captivates potential readers and compels them to dive into the pages of your book.

CHAPTER 7
THE POWER OF
FEEDBACK AND
ITERATION

YOU'VE POURED your heart and soul into crafting a compelling blurb that captures the essence of your book and entices potential readers. However, the work doesn't stop there. To ensure your blurb is as effective as possible, it's crucial to test, gather feedback, and refine your copy based on reader responses. In this chapter, we'll explore strategies for soliciting valuable input and using data-driven insights to optimise your blurb for maximum impact.

Just as you wouldn't publish your book without going through multiple rounds of editing and revisions, your blurb deserves the same level of attention and refinement. Testing your blurb allows you to:

- Gauge reader interest and engagement
- Identify areas of confusion or lack of clarity
- Determine which elements resonate most with your target audience
- Optimise your language and messaging for maximum impact

By actively seeking feedback and iterating based on reader responses, you can craft a blurb that not only captures attention but also effectively communicates the value and unique selling points of your book.

~

There are several ways to gather valuable feedback on your blurb.

Engage a group of beta readers who represent your target audience. Share your blurb with them and ask for their honest opinions. Provide a structured feedback form that includes questions such as, what intrigued them most about the blurb? Did it convey the book's genre and central themes? Was there anything confusing or unclear? Most importantly, after reading the blurb, how likely are they to buy the book on a scale of 1-10?

Analyse the responses and look for patterns or recurring comments. Use this feedback to identify areas for improvement and make necessary revisions.

A/B testing, also known as split testing, involves creating two versions of your blurb and comparing their performance. This data-driven approach allows you to determine which version resonates more with your target audience. Here's how to conduct an A/B test:

1. Create two variations of your blurb, changing specific elements such as the hook, the call to action, or the tone.
2. Use tools like Amazon Ads, Facebook Ads, or email marketing platforms to present each version to a segment of your target audience.

3. Monitor key metrics such as click-through rates, conversion rates, and engagement levels for each version.
4. Analyse the results to determine which version performed better and iterate accordingly.

A/B testing provides concrete data on the effectiveness of your blurb, helping you make informed decisions and optimise your copy for maximum impact.

Leverage your existing readership or author platform to gather feedback through surveys and polls. Share your blurb on social media, your author website, or your email newsletter, and ask readers to provide their opinions. Use tools like Google Forms, Survey Monkey, or social media polling features to create simple and engaging surveys.

Ask questions similar to those used for beta reader feedback, and encourage readers to provide open-ended comments or suggestions. Survey Monkey the responses to identify trends and insights that can guide your blurb refinement process.

$\sim$

Once you've gathered feedback through various channels, it's time to put those insights into action. Review the comments, suggestions, and data collected, and look for patterns or recurring themes.

Consider what resonated most with readers. Look for common points of confusion or lack of clarity. Did readers feel compelled to buy your book after reading the blurb? What suggestions or alternative phrases did you hear from your test groups?

Use these insights to make targeted revisions to your

blurb. Focus on enhancing the elements that worked well and addressing any areas of weakness or confusion. Be willing to experiment with different hooks, calls to action, and language choices based on reader feedback.

Crafting a killer blurb is not a one-and-done endeavour. It requires a commitment to testing, gathering feedback, and iterating based on reader responses. You may need to go through multiple rounds of testing and revision before arriving at the most effective version. Embrace the feedback loop and continue to seek input from your target audience as you fine-tune your copy.

A well-crafted, thoroughly tested, and refined blurb can be a powerful marketing asset that helps your book stand out in a crowded marketplace and attracts the right readers to your work.

CHAPTER 8

BLURB WRITING FOR BOOK SERIES

WHEN IT COMES to crafting blurbs for a book series, you'll face a unique set of challenges and opportunities.

Unlike stand-alone novels, series blurbs must not only entice new readers to dive into the story but also satisfy and engage existing fans who have followed the series from the beginning.

Writing blurbs for a book series comes with its own set of challenges. You need to avoid spoilers for previous books in the series. At the same time, you're forced to provide enough context for new readers without overwhelming them. Because your readers will have expectations from you as a writer, it's vital you focus on maintaining consistency in tone and style across the series. Highlight the unique elements of each instalment while emphasising the overarching series arc. You need to keep existing fans engaged and excited for the next book.

Navigating these challenges requires a strategic approach to blurb writing that considers the needs and expectations of both new and existing readers.

~

To draw in new readers who may not be familiar with your series, provide a brief introduction to the main characters and the world they inhabit. Focus on the most compelling aspects that will capture the interest of potential readers. Highlight unique features, such as an intriguing magic system, a dystopian society, or a charismatic protagonist.

Clearly communicate the central conflict or theme that drives the series. Whether it's a battle against an ancient evil, a quest for self-discovery, or a struggle for survival, make sure new readers understand the core premise and stakes involved.

While providing context for the series as a whole, also tease the unique elements or plot developments specific to the book you're promoting. This could be a new villain, an unexpected twist, or a significant character arc that sets this instalment apart.

Draw comparisons to popular series or authors in your genre to help new readers understand what they can expect. Use taglines or phrases that encapsulate the essence of your series and create a sense of intrigue or excitement.

~

To keep existing fans engaged and eager for the next instalment, without giving away major spoilers, acknowledge key events or character developments from previous books that have shaped the current story. This shows existing fans that their investment in the series is valued and that the new book builds upon the established foundation.

Tease the new challenges, obstacles, or personal growth that beloved characters will face in the upcoming book. Existing fans are invested in the characters' journeys, so hinting at significant developments or emotional stakes will pique their interest.

If your series features rich world-building or an intricate lore, mention how the new book expands upon or deepens these elements. Existing fans will be excited to learn more about the fictional universe they've come to love.

Ensure that the tone and style of your series blurbs remain consistent across all books. This consistency creates a sense of familiarity and trust for existing fans, reassuring them that they can expect the same level of quality and engagement they've come to associate with your series.

~

To strike a balance between attracting new readers and satisfying existing fans, use a mix of strategies from both categories, focusing on the most relevant and compelling aspects for each book. Craft a blurb that can stand alone for new readers while also offering Easter eggs or nods to existing fans.

Prioritise clarity and concision, avoiding excessive details or references that may confuse or alienate new readers. Consider creating multiple versions of your blurb, with one tailored for new readers and another for existing fans, and use them in different marketing channels. Engage with your existing fanbase to gather feedback and insights on what they'd like to see emphasised in your series blurbs.

While crafting blurbs for a book series presents unique challenges, it also offers significant opportunities. A well-written series blurb can attract a dedicated and loyal readership that eagerly anticipates each new release. Done right, it will create a sense of community and shared experience among readers who follow your series.

The blurb is key to your marketing efforts and a series blurb is the perfect place to generate buzz and word-of-mouth marketing as fans discuss and recommend your books to others. It should establish your series as a recognisable brand within your genre, increasing visibility and discoverability.

Above all else, it provides you with opportunities for cross-promotion and bundling of books within the series.

CHAPTER 9
COLLABORATING WITH PROFESSIONALS

AS AN AUTHOR, you pour your heart and soul into your book, crafting a story or sharing knowledge that you believe will captivate and inspire readers. However, when it comes to writing a compelling blurb that effectively markets your book, you may find yourself facing a new set of challenges. This is where collaborating with professional blurb writers, editors, and marketers can make a significant difference in refining and optimising your blurbs for maximum impact.

While some authors have a natural knack for writing persuasive copy, others may struggle to distil their book's essence into a few compelling paragraphs. If you're new to the publishing world, working with a professional can help you navigate the complexities of book marketing and ensure your blurb makes a strong first impression. If you're writing in a popular genre with many new releases, a professionally crafted blurb can help your book stand out from the crowd. If you're venturing into a new genre or targeting a different demographic, a professional can help you tailor your blurb to appeal to that specific audience. If you've been using a blurb that you wrote yourself but aren't seeing the sales or engagement you hoped for, it may be time to bring in a professional to help you refine and optimise your copy.

Collaborating with professional blurb writers, editors, and marketers can offer numerous advantages. Professionals who specialise in crafting blurbs have a deep understanding of what makes a blurb effective. They can draw upon their experience working with various genres, authors, and audiences to create copy that resonates.

Writing a great blurb takes time and effort. By collaborating with a professional, you can free up your time to focus on other aspects of your book launch or writing your next project.

As the author, you may be too close to your book to see it from a potential reader's perspective. A professional can provide an objective viewpoint and help you identify the most compelling aspects of your story or message. Professionals stay up-to-date with the latest trends and best practices in book marketing. They can ensure your blurb adheres to industry standards and incorporates proven techniques for engaging readers.

And just like with a professionally designed cover, a professionally crafted blurb stands out and can significantly increase your book's visibility, engagement, and sales potential. It can help you attract the right readers and establish a strong brand identity.

∼

If you've decided to collaborate with a professional to refine and optimise your blurb, here are some steps you can take to find the right partner and ensure a smooth working relationship:

Research and compare services: Look for blurb writing, editing, or marketing services that specialise in your genre or niche. Compare their portfolios, testimonials, and pricing to find the best fit for your needs and budget.

Provide clear information and expectations: When reaching out to a professional, provide detailed information about your book, target audience, and marketing goals. Be clear about your expectations and timeline for the project.

Communicate openly and actively take part: Collaboration is a two-way street. Be open to feedback and suggestions from the professional, and actively participate in the process by providing insights, answering questions, and reviewing drafts.

Trust their expertise: While it's essential to provide input and ensure the blurb aligns with your vision, trust the professional's expertise and experience. They may suggest changes or approaches that you hadn't considered but that can significantly enhance your blurb's effectiveness.

Provide feedback and iterate: After receiving the initial draft, provide constructive feedback and work with the professional to refine and iterate the blurb until it meets your expectations.

To make the most of your collaboration with a professional blurb writer, editor, or marketer, be open to new ideas and approaches: While you may have a specific vision for your blurb, be receptive to new ideas and perspectives that the professional brings to the table. The more information you can provide about your book, target audience, and unique selling points, the better equipped the professional will be to craft a compelling blurb.

Share examples of blurbs or marketing copy that resonate with you and align with your brand's tone and style. This will help the professional understand your preferences and create a blurb that feels authentic to your voice.

While a professionally crafted blurb can significantly improve your book's chances of success, it's not a cure-all. Set realistic expectations and understand that other factors, such as cover design, marketing efforts, and the quality of your book, also play crucial roles in your book's performance.

Consider working with a team of professionals, including cover designers, formatters, and marketers, to ensure your blurb is part of a cohesive and effective overall book marketing strategy.

Collaborating with professional blurb writers, editors, and marketers can be a game-changer for authors looking to refine and optimise their blurbs. By using their experience, objective perspective, and industry knowledge, you can create interesting copy that effectively engages your target audience and boosts your book's visibility and sales potential.

By communicating openly, actively taking part in the process, and trusting the professional's expertise, you can ensure a successful outcome that elevates your blurb and sets your book up for success.

CHAPTER 10
THE POWER OF BOOK
MARKETING

BEFORE HELPING WRITE your first blurb, I'd like to talk about book marketing as a whole. Everything hangs off one carefully crafted message, and often the blurb for your book serves as the brief for any marketing activity.

In the vast and competitive world of publishing, writing a great book is never enough to guarantee success. Think of how many big-selling authors brag about papering their bedroom walls with rejection letters.

Unlike advertising, which focuses on paid promotion, book marketing is more of an 'art'. It encompasses a wide range of strategies and techniques designed to organically raise awareness, generate buzz, and cultivate a loyal readership for your work.

As I said in the first chapter, to write a killer blurb, you need to understand your target audience. The foundation of effective book marketing also lies in understanding the readers most likely to connect with your book. What are their interests, preferences, and reading habits? By identifying your ideal reader, you can tailor your marketing efforts (and write a blurb) to reach them where they are, whether it's through social media, online communities, or in-person events.

Think of your book as an island. A lovely little island just off the coast of (let's say) Norway, with fabulous views, a couple of superb places to eat and plenty of Ingrammable hotspots. This island might be a well-kept secret. Just a handful of people know about it. They visit every year. They love it. They might tell a few friends, but that's it. The cafes on the island struggle to keep going - especially out of season and the local council just can't afford the upkeep. It doesn't help that the only way onto the island is by boat. And you need to know where to get this boat.

This island needs a bridge. Or at the very least a whole bunch of signposts telling people where to board the existing boat service. And because people won't just board a random boat to a random island they've never heard of before. A reason to take a punt on visiting this fabulous island. Because as anyone who's been there can confirm, once is never enough. When you've found the island, you'll return. Again and again.

Marketing helps people find the island. Marketing builds the bridge and the signpost to the boat service. Marketing puts together words and reasons for people to come and wish they'd come sooner.

This is what your blurb does.

This is why book marketing matters.

But staying with the Norwegian island theme - stick with me, I promise I'll find a different metaphor in the next chapter - who would be the ideal visitor? Who would love the island? And who would hate every second of their visit?

You need to think of your book in the same way.

To gain insights into your target reader, you need to carry out market research.

And that doesn't mean paying some vastly over-hyped consultancy company to produce a bunch of pretty Power-Point presentations and graphs. You need to sit down with a pen and paper - and access to the Internet - and do some thinking.

The best place to start is by thinking about why you wrote this book. Who were your influences? Did you write the book to solve someone's problems or because you loved reading something in the same vein or because you had a story to tell and loved how another writer told their tales? Unless you're incredibly niche, there will be lots of other books just like yours - or not exactly like yours, but your book will sit in what we call a 'genre'. It might be a fantasy, a romance, sci-fi, or a how-to manual.

Go online (or nip to a bookshop) and analyse the current bestselling books in your genre. Read how they present themselves and try to imagine who might want to read them. See if you can work out the demographics and Psychographics of their readers. Search online for forums and book clubs or websites about your specialist subject. Read social media posts, all the time taking notes to understand the needs and desires of people who read books like the one you've written.

~

A phrase that's been done to death is 'author platform'. You'll keep hearing how you absolutely must have a strong online presence. And yes, it probably does help. But for fiction writers, only if you've written a few books. It matters far more if you're trying to sell a non-fiction book.

Then you need to find ways to engage in online discussions that lend your persona credibility in any field.

If you're a first-strike fiction writer, you don't need a website. You don't need to be on any of the social media channels - trust me, nobody sells books by shouting about them on X. However, because I know writers are a stubborn lot who refuse to believe every word they read, let's pretend for a minute that it matters more than anything else.

And, in the world of blurb writing, having a website can help you distil ideas, so why not go for it?

AN AUTHOR WEBSITE

You can do this so easily these days and you don't need to be a technical whizz-kid or pay an agency big bucks to build you something. There are several free and user-friendly options available that make it easy to create a professional-looking website with no coding experience.

WordPress.com: WordPress.com offers a free plan that allows you to create a basic website with limited customisation options. It's user-friendly and offers a wide range of templates to choose from.

Wix: Wix provides an intuitive drag-and-drop interface that makes it easy to create a visually appealing website. They offer a free plan with limited features and Wix branding.

· · ·

Weebly: Weebly is another user-friendly option that offers a free plan with basic features. It provides a simple drag-and-drop editor and a variety of templates to choose from.

When creating your first author website, keep it simple.

Home Page: Your home page should provide a brief introduction to who you are as an author and what your book is about. Include a compelling headline, a short bio, and an eye-catching image of your book cover.

About Page: Use this page to share a more detailed author bio, including your background, writing journey, and any relevant credentials or awards. Include a professional headshot to help readers put a face to your name.

Books Page: Dedicate a page to showcasing your book(s). Include the book cover image, a synopsis, and links to purchase your book from various retailers (e.g., Amazon, Barnes & Noble, or your online store).

Contact Page: Make it easy for readers, media, or potential collaborators to get in touch with you. Include a contact form or provide an email address where they can reach you. You can also include links to your social media profiles.

· · ·

Blog (Optional): Consider starting a blog where you can share your thoughts, writing tips, or behind-the-scenes insights into your book. This can help you engage with your readers and establish yourself as an authority in your genre. If you're writing fiction though, your time might be better spent not doing this.

When designing your website, keep it simple and visually appealing. Choose a clean, easy-to-read font and a colour scheme that complements your book cover or genre. Use high-quality images that reflect your brand and the tone of your book.

Most website builders offer free templates you can customise to suit your needs. Choose a template that aligns with your genre and provides a clear navigation structure. Make sure that your website is mobile-friendly, as many readers will access it from their smartphones or tablets.

SOCIAL MEDIA

Some writers love 'the socials'. Others hate the time it takes to stay on top of so many feeds or make sure you're doing the right thing on the right site. Most authors will tell you they can't honestly prove that posting something on their socials has generated a proven sale of a book.

At the same time, I can't deny that almost everyone is doing it in some form or another. I sometimes use it to shout about a book. Other times, I let off steam. It's not the worst place to go for ideas if you need to find someone crazy and work out what makes them tick.

While not every author needs to be active on every social media platform, I can't deny that having a presence on one or two key platforms can significantly affect your book's visibility and success.

The key is deciding which one or two you like can work with and want to maintain. And again, some of this choice has to be driven by what you've found out about your target audience.

Everything I'm going to say now sort of only applies after you've chosen your platforms and built an audience. If you have 100 followers, it's not going to be particularly useful. There are loads of other books and websites that will tell you how to grow your online followers. I'm not aiming to do that in this particular book.

Where social media helps with blurb writing is, it's a place to try out different versions of how you talk about your work. For free. Post ten different hook lines over time. Which do people like or share? Which generates adverse reactions?

Social media platforms provide a direct line of communication between authors and readers. You can interact with your audience, respond to their comments and questions, and gather valuable feedback about your book.

By consistently sharing content that resonates with your target audience, you can demonstrate your unique voice, personality, and expertise in your genre, making it easier for readers to connect with you and your work. Building relationships with readers can foster a sense of loyalty and encourage them to become advocates for your work.

One area that does work well for authors is networking with the Writing Community: Social media allows you to connect with fellow authors, industry professionals, and book bloggers. Building relationships within the writing community can lead to valuable opportunities, such as guest blog posts, author interviews, or collaborative promotions, which can help expose your book to new audiences.

But again - don't just use it to post 'buy my book' notices. Nobody will.

EMAIL NEWSLETTERS

Build an email list of engaged readers who are interested in your work. Regularly send newsletters featuring book updates, exclusive content, and special offers to nurture your relationship with your subscribers and keep them informed about your latest projects.

Again, here is where you can test out blurbs. If you have two versions. Try sending them to your readers and ask which one they like. By involving your readers, you build brand loyalty and also get free feedback from actual readers.

LEVERAGING BOOK REVIEWS AND ENDORSEMENTS

Book reviews and endorsements serve as powerful social proof, influencing potential readers' decisions to purchase your book. Seek out reviews from respected sources, such as popular book bloggers, literary publications, or industry experts. A positive review from a trusted source can lend credibility to your work and encourage readers to take a chance on your book.

And this is something to tag onto the end of any great book blurb.

But be aware, when you pitch your work to these people, they'll need to know what it is they're expected to read - so the blurb matters even more.

~

Literary PR (public relations) plays a vital role in book marketing, helping authors gain media exposure, build credibility, and reach a wider audience. PR professionals specialise in crafting compelling press releases, pitching stories to journalists and bloggers, and securing media placements for authors.

They can help write a great blurb - but it helps if you have one ready to go. Mostly because it's going to save you money. Money you can use to ask a publicist to help promote your work on a wider stage.

Book marketing is not a one-time event but an ongoing process that requires persistence, patience, and a long-term perspective. Building a loyal readership and establishing yourself as a successful author takes time and consistent effort.

Embrace the long game by consistently engaging with

your audience, producing valuable content, and nurturing relationships with readers, fellow authors, and industry professionals. Celebrate your successes, learn from your setbacks, and stay committed to your craft and your marketing efforts.

Remember, book marketing is not about hard selling but about creating meaningful connections, providing value, and building a community around your work. By authentically engaging with your readers, understanding their needs, and delivering exceptional content, you can cultivate a devoted fan base that will support you throughout your writing career.

In the next chapter, I'll dive deeper into the art of crafting compelling blurbs that captivate readers and drive book sales. From understanding the key components of a killer blurb to mastering the language and structure that hooks readers.

CHAPTER 11
THE POWER OF KEYWORDS AND METADATA

IN THE EVER-EVOLVING DIGITAL LANDSCAPE, authors and publishers are being forced to adapt their strategies to ensure their books stand out amidst a sea of online content. Whether you know your iPad from your processor speeds or if the very thought of going online fills you with terror, this is a chapter you can't afford to skip. But I'll try to stay away from the jargon - as far as possible.

Keywords are specific words or phrases that potential readers might use when searching for a book like yours online. They can include topics, themes, genres, character archetypes, or any other relevant terms associated with your book.

Metadata refers to the information that describes your book, such as the title, author name, publisher, ISBN, publication date, and category. Metadata also encompasses your book's description, which is where your blurb comes into play. A lot of this is set up by the publisher (which might be you) and appears to be completely disconnected from writing the blurb. It isn't.

When a reader searches for a book online, search engines and book retailer algorithms use keywords and metadata to determine the relevance and ranking of search results. By strategically incorporating keywords into your blurb and optimising your metadata, you increase the chances of your book appearing in front of the right audience.

～

To identify the most effective keywords for your book, you'll need to conduct thorough research.

Start by listing words and phrases that accurately describe your book's content, genre, themes, and target audience. Consider the terms you would use to search for your book online. Look at the blurbs and metadata of books similar to yours. Note the keywords they use and consider incorporating them into your blurb, if relevant.

There are tools out there that will help you find the right keywords that people search on when looking for their next book.

By far the easiest way to find this is to open an 'incognito' or private browser window. We do this so your search isn't polluted by things you've looked for in the past. Go to your local Amazon website and type a word into the search far. A word related to your book like 'romance'. See what other 'autofill' words crop up. Then type those in. Keep a note of them all.

There are a bunch of free 'plug-ins' that you can add to your browser - especially if you use Chrome. I recommend 'Kindletrends'. It provides insights and data to improve a book's discoverability and visibility in Amazon's search results. The plug-in helps identify high-performing keywords relevant to a book's genre, topic, and target audience. It provides data on keyword search volume, competition, and potential rankings. Kindletrends analyses the categories and subcategories on Amazon, helping select the most appropriate and competitive categories for your book.

When you find a book a little like the one you're writing or about to sell, look at the "Customers Also Bought" list, along with the "Customers Also Viewed". Read the blurbs that power these books into the hands of readers.

Once you have identified your target keywords, the next step is to incorporate them naturally into your book blurb. While it's important to include keywords, your blurb should still read smoothly and engage potential readers. Avoid overloading your blurb with keywords to the point where it becomes clunky or unnatural.

Aim to include your primary keywords in the opening sentence or paragraph of your blurb, as this can carry more weight with search algorithms. However, be sure that the placement feels organic and not forced. To avoid repetition and maintain a natural flow, use variations of your keywords or synonyms throughout your blurb. This helps cover a broader range of search queries while keeping your blurb engaging.

If your book has a unique angle or selling point that aligns with a specific keyword, put it up front in your blurb. This can help your book stand out from competitors targeting similar keywords.

In addition to your blurb, the metadata associated with your book plays a significant role in its discoverability. One trick many authors use these days is they use a subtitle that adds to the 'discoverability' of their book. One word of warning, if you go down this path, don't think about changing it too often. It leads to broken links on some book store pages - and Amazon flips its lid if you do it too often.

Select the most relevant categories and genres for your book when listing it on retailer sites or in metadata databases. In addition to your blurb, many platforms allow you to input separate keywords or tags associated with your book. Use this opportunity to include relevant terms that didn't fit naturally into your blurb.

~

Discoverability is an ongoing process, and it's essential to monitor your book's performance and make adjustments as needed. Regularly check your book's rankings on retailer sites and in relevant category lists. Note any changes or fluctuations in rankings and consider adjusting your keywords or metadata accordingly.

Use tools like Google Analytics or Amazon Author Central to gain insights into the search terms readers are using to find your book. Identify any new or unexpected keywords that you could incorporate into your blurb or metadata.

Pay attention to reader reviews and feedback, both on retailer sites and social media. Look for common themes or phrases that readers use to describe your book, and consider incorporating them into your keywords or blurb.

Don't be afraid to experiment with different keywords, blurb variations, or metadata optimisations. Make small changes and monitor their impact on your book's discoverability and sales. Continuously refine your approach based on data and insights.

CHAPTER 12
PUFF PIECES

LET'S go beyond the blurb itself. Beyond the bit where someone tells someone else what the book they might buy is about.

Most every book comes with an endorsement - often the words of some other famous and much-loved author or someone who knows their stuff when it comes to recommending and writing novels or books about how to put up shelves.

Sometimes these people have read the book in question. Often they may have flicked through the opening chapters just to get an idea and make sure they're not attaching their name to a big pile of steaming nonsense. Usually, they've been told to write something by their agent or publisher. Back-scratching is commonplace.

As - I assume - an author with low clout when it comes to guilt-tripping other authors to write 'puff pieces', you may need to be creative with how you pad out your blurb with reader recommendations. After all, we all like to think that we're buying something that other people like. We want to read books with merit. If an author we love has said a book is great, chances are we'll trust them.

Publishers, big-time magazine and newspaper reviewers and bookstore buyers set great store by puff pieces. One in the hand is worth three in the wild.

The most important thing to remember about these puff piece blurbs is they don't just appear. Someone (and that someone is almost certainly you) needs to go out and find them.

Unless you hit lucky and write a convincing begging letter to your favourite author - and it arrives right when they're taking a break from writing their next big seller - your best bet is to throw yourself into the bear pit that is *Good Reads* or scour your Amazon reviews. If you truly want to indulge in self-harm, turn to social media. Ask random strangers what they think.

There is another path to follow if your bank account is just too full of money. Serious literary journals like Publishers Weekly, Kirkus Reviews and the like will happily take £500 off you in exchange for the sort of review that does carry clout. But only if the professional getting paid to read your (often self-published) work is impressed. Don't even think of investing in this if you haven't also paid out for a professional cover design and several rounds of professional editing - it's not enough to have had your best friend read your manuscript and then run it through Grammarly.

Some sites allow you to post your books online weeks or months ahead of publication and invite people to download them (for free) with the hope they might post a review. One of the better-known examples - at least in the UK - is NetGalley. Be warned. This isn't a cheap option. And you are giving away copies of your book. Nobody who downloads it is obliged to post a review - most of them won't even read it. There is a strange breed of browser that collects e-books and never opens them.

There is an expectation that anyone who downloads your book from one of these sites does review it and that they post the review somewhere it can be easily found - like Amazon or *Good Reads*. Again, they might. They might not. And you might wish they didn't.

You usually will receive a list of everyone who downloaded the book along with their email address and you are permitted to email these people once (at most twice) and politely suggest they review your work.

If the review is awful and they only post it on NetGalley, it's best to leave well enough alone. You will never be able to get this review removed. Don't even try. If you do, there's a chance they might also post it elsewhere. A NetGalley review is unlikely to ever be seen by people paying actual money out for actual books.

But if the review is good or even great. Use it to promote your book. Edit your back copy blurb:

"A billion times better than anything Shakespeare ever wrote…" - **NetGalley Review**

~

Most times, book buyers scan in a certain order. They look at the cover. They may take in the title. If they've heard of you, your author name registers, otherwise, not. And then they scan the blurb. But they scan it in a certain order. The first thing they look for are the bold-typed puff pieces. The reviews. Who else said this is a good book? And then, they might read the summary blurb that you've spent weeks perfecting with the help of this very volume.

Often our first encounter with a book is a pull quote plastered across the front cover - words of fulsome praise from someone who matters. And if that reviewer has avoided the bog-standard cliches of 'page-turner' or 'couldn't put it down' then that's all to the good. Nothing says 'contractual obligation to puff' like these stock phrases.

And because you'll hear this in trying to assemble a puff quote, often in the publishing industry these words of praise also find themselves referred to as 'blurbs'.

CHAPTER 13
TRIGGER WARNINGS

IN RECENT YEARS, the concept of trigger warnings has gained increasing attention in the world of literature. They are brief statements that alert readers to potentially distressing or sensitive content within a book, such as graphic violence, sexual assault, or mental health issues. While some argue trigger warnings are essential for creating a safe and inclusive reading experience, others believe they may spoil the story or coddle readers. In this chapter, I'll explore the complexities of including trigger warnings in books and blurbs, and guide how to approach this potentially delicate topic.

At their core, trigger warnings should empower readers by giving them the information they need to make informed decisions about the content they consume. For individuals who have experienced trauma or struggle with mental health issues, certain themes or descriptions in a book may trigger intense emotional responses, panic attacks, or even relapses. By including a trigger warning, authors and publishers demonstrate respect for their readers' well-being and allow them to prepare themselves emotionally or choose to avoid the content altogether.

It's essential to recognise trigger warnings are not intended to censor content or restrict creative freedom. They should serve as a tool for readers to self-regulate and engage with the material on their terms. As an author, it's crucial to balance providing necessary warnings and preserving the integrity of your storytelling or to protect the integrity of your argument.

When considering whether to include a trigger warning, start by closely examining your book's content. Some common triggers include:

- Graphic violence or gore
- Sexual assault or abuse
- Child abuse or neglect
- Suicide or self-harm
- Eating disorders
- Substance abuse
- Mental health issues (e.g., depression, anxiety, PTSD)
- Hate speech or discrimination

Keep in mind that this list is not exhaustive, and what makes up a trigger can vary from person to person. If you're unsure whether a particular theme or scene warrants a warning, consider consulting with sensitivity readers or mental health professionals who can provide guidance.

Although this is primarily a book about writing a killer blurb, you may be asked to include such a warning on the cover of your book. My preference is that if asked to include such a warning, I would place it only on the standard copyright page. But you may not have that option and trends change.

Once you've identified potential triggers in your book, the next step is to craft a clear and concise warning. Aim to provide enough information to help readers make an informed decision without giving away key plot points or spoilers.

Consider the following tips:

- Be specific: Instead of using vague terms like "mature content," name the specific triggers, such as "contains depictions of sexual assault and self-harm."
- Avoid judgment: Present the information in a neutral, non-judgmental tone. Trigger warnings are not meant to imply that the content is inherently bad or wrong.
- Place warnings strategically: Trigger warnings are most effective when placed at the beginning of the book, such as on the copyright page or in the front matter. They can also be included in the book's description or blurb, particularly if the triggering content is a central theme.
- Consider formatting: To ensure visibility, consider setting the trigger warning apart from the main text using bold or italic formatting, or by placing it in a bordered box.

Here's an example of a well-crafted trigger warning:

Trigger Warning: This book contains graphic depictions of domestic violence and sexual assault.

Including trigger warnings in your book's blurb can be a bit trickier, as you have limited space to convey the essential elements of your story while also providing necessary content warnings. However, if your book deals heavily with potentially triggering themes, it's crucial to mention them upfront to attract the right readership and avoid blind-siding sensitive readers.

When incorporating trigger warnings into your blurb, I strongly suggest you try to weave them in organically rather than tacking them on as an afterthought. Consider the following examples:

Example 1 (without trigger warning): Sarah thought she had escaped her traumatic past, but when she returns to her home town, old demons resurface, threatening to destroy everything she holds dear.

Example 2 (with trigger warning): Sarah thought she had escaped her traumatic past, but when she returns to her home town, old demons resurface. As she confronts the abuse she suffered as a child, Sarah must find the strength to break free from the cycle of violence and reclaim her life. *(Contains depictions of child abuse and domestic violence.)*

In the second example, the trigger warning flows naturally from the blurb's content, giving readers a clearer sense of what to expect without feeling abrupt or jarring.

~

Ultimately, the decision to include trigger warnings is a personal one that each author must make based on their artistic vision, target audience, and the specific content of their book. You may also find yourself expected to do this depending on your publisher or the community identified as your target audience. It's why knowing who you expect to buy your book is fundamental to getting the blurb and marketing copy spot on.

While some may argue that trigger warnings diminish the impact of storytelling or spoil the reading experience, they serve a vital purpose for many readers.

As creators, we have a responsibility to consider the diverse needs and experiences of our readership. By providing trigger warnings, we demonstrate empathy, respect, and a commitment to fostering an inclusive literary community where everyone feels safe and supported.

CHAPTER 14
GOOD BLURB, BAD BLURB

BY NOW, you'll be on board with me. Writing an engaging blurb is an essential skill for authors and marketers alike, as it serves as the primary marketing copy to attract readers and convince them to spend money on a book. Whether you're crafting a blurb for fiction or non-fiction, the principles of clear, compelling, and concise writing apply. In this chapter, we'll explore what makes a great blurb, provide examples of effective and ineffective blurbs (some of which I've had to create to show you how NOT to do it), and discuss the elements that contribute to their success or failure.

We already looked at the elements of a great blurb: the hook, synopsis, emotional appeal, unique selling point and call to action.

GOOD BLURBS

Ditch the mistletoe and fruitcake and prepare for this big-hearted holiday romp. Amidst all the revelry, a down-on-his-luck department store Santa and an out-of-work waitress find laughter, light, and self-discovery on a gay cruise. This holiday, get ready to be entertained by a tale of love, self-acceptance, and living authentically.

Why it works:

- The hook ("Ditch the mistletoe and fruitcake") is playful and immediately sets a light, humorous tone.
- It introduces the main characters and a unique setting—a gay cruise—adding intrigue.
- It connects emotionally by promising themes of self-acceptance and authenticity.
- The call to action is implicit, inviting the reader to join in the revelry.
- It doesn't end on a question - and it so easily could have.

With startups facing a fiercely competitive funding environment, 'The Art of Startup Fundraising' offers a lifeline. This thought-provoking book pulls back the Silicon Valley curtain to reveal how to secure the capital your startup needs to thrive. Discover insider strategies and expert advice in this essential guide to making smart, impactful financial decisions.

Why it works:

- Begins with a relevant and engaging hook about the competitive nature of startup funding.
- Clearly outlines the book's value proposition—insider strategies for fundraising.
- Provides a strong emotional appeal by positioning the book as a "lifeline."
- Encourages action with promises of essential guidance.

On a warm summer morning in North Carthage, Missouri, it is Nick and Amy Dunne's fifth wedding anniversary. Presents are being wrapped and reservations are being made when Nick's clever and beautiful wife disappears from their rented mansion on the Mississippi River. Husband-of-the-year Nick isn't doing himself any favours with cringe-worthy daydreams about the slope and shape of his wife's head, but passages from Amy's diary suggest a sinister darkness at the core of their marriage. This masterful novel takes readers inside a marriage that is as hollow as it appears to be perfect.

Why it works:

- The hook is strong, presenting a dramatic and intriguing scenario—the disappearance of Nick's wife.
- It offers a glimpse into the complex dynamics between the characters, hinting at dark undercurrents.
- The blurb sets up a mystery that promises to delve into the psychological and emotional depths of a troubled marriage.
- It ends with a statement that suggests a gripping read, enticing readers to dive into the story to uncover the truth.

In this generation-defining self-help guide, the writer cuts through the crap to show us a counter-intuitive approach to living a good life. Manson advises us to get to know our limitations and accept them. This is a refreshing slap for a generation to help them lead contented, grounded lives.

Why it works:

- The hook immediately captures attention with its bold language and clear, unconventional thesis.
- It clearly articulates the book's unique approach to self-help, challenging conventional wisdom.
- The emotional appeal is direct, presenting the book as a necessary corrective for contemporary life.
- The call to action is implicit, promising practical advice that can lead to a more fulfilling life.

The circus arrives without warning. No announcements precede it. It is simply there. When yesterday it was not. Within the black-and-white striped canvas tents is an utterly unique experience full of breathtaking amazements. It is called Le Cirque des Rêves, and it is only open at night. But behind the scenes, a fierce competition is underway—a duel between two young magicians, Celia and Marco, who have been trained since childhood expressly for this purpose by their mercurial instructors. Unbeknownst to them, this is a game in which only one can be left standing, and the circus is but the stage for a remarkable battle of imagination and will.

Why it works:

- The hook ("The circus arrives without warning.") is mysterious and intriguing, instantly capturing the reader's attention.
- The blurb skillfully sets the scene with vivid descriptions that promise a unique and magical experience.
- It introduces the central conflict and stakes clearly, adding layers of intrigue.
- The emotional appeal is woven through the depiction of the setting and the stakes involved in the competition, inviting readers to immerse themselves in the novel's magical world.

Born to survivalists in the mountains of Idaho, the author was seventeen the first time she set foot in a class-

room. Her quest for knowledge transformed her, taking her over oceans and across continents, to Harvard and Cambridge University. Only then would she wonder if she had travelled too far and if there was still a way home. A riveting account of self-invention and the struggle for a sense of belonging and understanding in a complex world.

Why it works:

- The hook immediately sets up an extraordinary personal narrative ("Born to survivalists in the mountains of Idaho...").
- It succinctly outlines the transformative journey of the author, which is both inspiring and compelling.
- The emotional appeal is strong, focusing on the universal themes of belonging, identity, and the power of education.
- The blurb promises a deep, introspective look at the author's life, encouraging readers to explore her remarkable story.

BAD BLURBS

Follow Captain Ahab as he sails the seas on his ship, the Pequod, with his crew, hunting the white whale, Moby Dick, who once bit off his leg. Experience life on the sea and the pursuit of an obsession.

Why it fails:

- The hook lacks the emotional and thematic depth that defines the novel; it merely describes the plot with no allure.
- It fails to capture the philosophical and existential queries that are central to the narrative.
- There is no mention of the rich symbolism or the complex character dynamics that engage the reader beyond the surface-level adventure.
- The blurb does not evoke curiosity or offer a compelling reason to delve into this classic tale of obsession and revenge.

Join Santiago, a young shepherd boy, as he travels from his home in Spain to the Egyptian desert in search of a treasure buried near the Pyramids. Along the way, he meets interesting people and faces various challenges.

Why it fails:

- The hook is simplistic and does not reflect the philosophical depth or the spiritual journey that the book promises.
- It summarises the journey without highlighting the transformative experiences or the mystical elements that are key to the narrative's appeal.
- Lacks an emotional pull; it does not connect the reader to the protagonist's inner quest or the larger existential questions explored in the book.

- It misses a call to action or a compelling reason to follow Santiago's journey, making the blurb feel flat and uninspired.

Follow Pi Patel as he survives on a lifeboat with a Bengal tiger named Richard Parker after their ship sinks in the Pacific. They face many challenges on the open sea.

Why it fails:

- The hook is straightforward but fails to capture the philosophical depth or the emotional intensity of the novel.
- It summarises the plot without creating intrigue or highlighting the novel's unique aspects.
- The blurb does not engage with the reader on an emotional level or suggest the broader themes of survival, faith, and truth.
- It lacks a persuasive call to action, merely describing events without selling the reader on the experience of the novel.

This novel is the story of a man who said that he would stop the motor of the world—and did. Tremendous in scope, and breathtaking in its suspense, Atlas Shrugged stretches the boundaries of the novel to reveal what can happen in a society that ceases to reward creative energy and vision. Has there ever been anyone like him before or since?

Why it fails:

- The hook is vague and does not adequately convey the novel's premise or stakes.
- It lacks specific details about the plot or characters that might engage the reader's interest.
- The blurb promises an exploration of societal themes but does not offer a compelling emotional or intellectual appeal.
- It does not clearly articulate why a reader should care about the narrative or what they stand to gain from reading it.
- The question - oh my, the question.

This book covers all aspects of real estate practices in the modern era. It discusses various topics such as buying, selling, and leasing properties.

Why it fails:

- The hook is non-existent; it simply states the topic with no engaging element.
- The synopsis is too broad and does not specify why this book is different or necessary.
- Lacks emotional connection; it does not relate to the reader's challenges or goals.
- No clear call to action.

A great blurb should make the reader feel compelled to discover more about the book. By employing a strong hook, a clear and intriguing synopsis, an emotional appeal, and a persuasive call to action, authors can significantly increase their book's attractiveness and sales potential. Reviewing examples of successful and unsuccessful blurbs helps in understanding these dynamics and refining the approach to blurb writing.

ADDITIONAL MATERIAL

Much of what follows has a focus on fiction, though the concepts apply also to non-fiction writing. They consider popular ways of shaping and planning stories and how you can take from these structures and plot structures to feed your synopsis and build a killer blurb.

ADDITIONAL MATERIAL

CHECKLISTS

Fiction:

1. Introduce the protagonist(s) and establish the setting and time period early on.
2. Clearly convey the protagonist's motivations and goals.
3. Identify the genre and ensure the tone and plot elements are consistent with reader expectations.
4. Mention the inciting incident that propels the protagonist into action and disrupts the status quo.
5. Highlight the main conflicts and challenges the protagonist faces, both external and internal.
6. Emphasise the high stakes and the consequences of failure for the protagonist.
7. Tease the central mystery, question, or problem without giving away the resolution.
8. Use engaging, active language that captures the essence of the story.

9. Ensure the blurb accurately reflects the story's content and tone.
10. Keep the blurb concise, typically around 150-200 words.

Non-Fiction:

1. Begin with a compelling hook, such as a startling statistic, provocative question, personal anecdote, bold claim, or description of a problem.
2. Clearly state the main argument, theme, or purpose of the book.
3. Highlight the key benefits or takeaways for the reader.
4. Identify the target audience and explain why the book applies to them.
5. Establish the author's credibility and expertise on the subject matter.
6. Mention any unique features of the book, such as groundbreaking research, exclusive interviews, or practical exercises.
7. Use persuasive language that conveys the value and importance of the book's content.
8. Include endorsements or testimonials from respected figures in the field, if available.
9. Ensure the blurb accurately represents the book's content and tone.
10. Keep the blurb concise, typically around 150-200 words.

General:

1. Use strong, active verbs and vivid, evocative language.
2. Avoid clichés, generalities, and overused phrases.
3. Use short paragraphs and bullet points for readability.
4. Format the blurb attractively, with appropriate font sizes and line spacing.
5. Proofread carefully for spelling, grammar, and punctuation errors.
6. Read the blurb aloud to ensure it flows smoothly and sounds engaging.
7. Show the blurb to others for feedback and make revisions as needed.
8. Ensure the blurb aligns with the overall design and aesthetics of the book cover.
9. Consider including a brief author bio or relevant endorsements.
10. Treat the blurb as a sales pitch and a promise to the reader, ensuring it accurately represents the book and entices them to read more.

A NOTE ON COPYRIGHT

When crafting your back cover blurb, it's important to be aware of legal considerations, particularly regarding the use of quotes or endorsements from other sources.

If you want to include a quote from another author's work or a review from a publication in your blurb, you ensure that you have permission, or that the use falls under the doctrine of *fair use*. Fair use allows limited use of copyrighted material without permission for purposes such as criticism, commentary, or promotion. However, the line between fair use and infringement can be blurry. To err on the side of caution, it's best to seek permission from the copyright holder before using their words in your blurb. This may involve contacting the author, publisher, or publication and getting written consent.

Including endorsements or testimonials from other authors, experts, or readers in your blurb can lend credibility and attract potential readers. However, it's crucial to ensure that these endorsements are accurate, truthful, and used with permission. Before featuring an endorsement, reach out to the person or entity providing the testimonial and get their explicit consent to use their words and name on your book cover. Be transparent about how their endorsement will be used and provide them with the opportunity to review the final version of the blurb. If you have any financial or personal relationships with the endorsers that could be seen as a conflict of interest, it's advisable to disclose that information to maintain transparency.

While copyright issues and the use of endorsements are important considerations, they should not deter you from creating an interesting and effective back cover blurb. By being proactive, seeking necessary permissions, and maintaining open communication with the parties involved, you can navigate these legal aspects with confidence.

If you have any doubts or concerns about the legal implications of your blurb content, it's always wise to consult with a legal professional specialising in intellectual property rights or publishing law. They can provide guidance specific to your situation and help you ensure that your blurb is both legally compliant and effective in promoting your book.

APPENDIX 1: THE HERO'S JOURNEY

The Hero's Journey, a storytelling structure popularised by Joseph Campbell, has been widely used in literature and film to create compelling narratives. This structure can also be leveraged to craft effective book blurbs that entice readers and give them a glimpse of the story's essence. By distilling the key elements of the Hero's Journey into a concise blurb, authors can pique the interest of potential readers and convey the emotional arc of their story.

Here's how you can use the Hero's Journey to create an effective book blurb:

1. Introduce the Ordinary World and the Hero Begin your blurb by briefly introducing the protagonist and their ordinary world. This sets the stage for the journey to come and helps readers connect with the hero. For example: "In a quiet suburban town, John Smith leads a simple life as a high school teacher."

2. Hint at the Call to Adventure and the Hero's Reluctance Next, allude to the event or challenge that disrupts the hero's ordinary world and sets them on their journey. This is known as the Call to Adventure. Often, the hero is reluctant to accept this call, and mentioning this reluctance can add intrigue to your blurb. For example: "But when a mysterious letter arrives, John is forced to confront a secret from his past – one he'd rather leave buried."

3. Tease the Challenges and Allies As the hero embarks on their journey, they will face many obstacles and meet allies who will aid them in their quest. In your blurb, tease these challenges and supporting characters without giving away too much. For example: "With the help of an unlikely ally, John must navigate a treacherous web of deceit and danger to uncover the truth."

4. Hint at the Hero's Inner Transformation Throughout the journey, the hero undergoes a profound inner transformation as they face their fears and overcome personal weaknesses. Hinting at this transformation in your blurb can give readers a sense of the emotional depth of your story. For example: "As he delves deeper into the mystery, John is forced to confront his demons and question everything he believes."

5. Allude to the Story's Climax and Resolution Finally, allude to the story's climax and the hero's ultimate triumph or failure, without spoiling the ending. This creates a sense of anticipation and leaves readers eager to discover how the story unfolds. For example: "In a race against time, John must make an impossible choice that will determine not only his fate but the fate of those he holds dear."

Here's an example of a complete blurb using the Hero's Journey structure:

"In a quiet suburban town, John Smith leads a simple life as a high school teacher. But when a mysterious letter arrives, John is forced to confront a secret from his past – one he'd rather leave buried. With the help of an unlikely ally, John must navigate a treacherous web of deceit and danger to uncover the truth. As he delves deeper into the mystery, John is forced to confront his own demons and question everything he believes. In a race against time, John must make an impossible choice that will determine not only his fate but the fate of those he holds dear."

By using the Hero's Journey as a guide, you can create a blurb that captures the essence of your story, hints at the emotional journey of your protagonist, and leaves readers eager to embark on the adventure alongside your hero.

APPENDIX 2: FREYTAG'S PYRAMID

Freytag's Pyramid, a dramatic structure developed by German novelist and playwright Gustav Freytag, has been widely used to analyse and create compelling stories. This structure can also craft effective book blurbs that capture the essence of a story and entice potential readers. By understanding the key elements of Freytag's Pyramid and how they relate to a story's narrative arc, authors can create blurbs that showcase the tension, conflict, and resolution of their tales.

Here's how you can use Freytag's Pyramid to create an effective book blurb:

1. Exposition: Set the Stage Begin your blurb by introducing the main characters and setting the stage for the story. This is known as the exposition, where you provide the background information to orient the reader. For example: "In the heart of New York City, detective Sarah Thompson is known for her keen instincts and unwavering dedication to justice."

2. Inciting Incident: Introduce the Conflict Next, introduce the inciting incident – the event that disrupts the status quo and sets the story's conflict in motion. This is the catalyst that propels the characters into action and raises the stakes. For example: "When a high-profile murder rocks the city, Sarah finds herself entangled in a case that threatens to unravel everything she holds dear."

3. Rising Action: Tease the Escalating Tension As the story progresses, the tension and conflict escalate, leading to the rising action. In your blurb, hint at the challenges and obstacles the characters face as they navigate the increasingly complex situation. For example: "As Sarah delves deeper into the investigation, she uncovers a web of corruption that reaches the highest levels of power, putting her own life on the line."

4. Climax: Hint at the Moment of Truth The climax is the pivotal moment in the story where the conflict reaches its peak, and the characters face their ultimate test. In your blurb, allude to this moment of truth without giving away the outcome. For example: "In a heart-pounding show-down, Sarah must confront the killer and make a choice that will forever change the course of her life."

5. Denouement: Tease the Resolution Finally, hint at the story's resolution, known as the denouement, without spoiling the ending. This gives readers a sense of closure and leaves them curious about how the characters' journeys conclude. For example: "As the dust settles, Sarah must come to terms with the consequences of her actions and the price of justice in a city where nothing is as it seems."

Here's an example of a complete blurb using Freytag's Pyramid:

> *"In the heart of New York City, detective Sarah Thompson is known for her keen instincts and unwavering dedication to justice. When a high-profile murder rocks the city, Sarah finds herself entangled in a case that threatens to unravel everything she holds dear. As she delves deeper into the investigation, she uncovers a web of corruption that reaches the highest levels of power, putting her own life on the line. In a heart-pounding showdown, Sarah must confront the killer and make a choice that will forever change the course of her life. As the dust settles, Sarah must come to terms with the consequences of her actions and the price of justice in a city where nothing is as it seems."*

By structuring your blurb around the key elements of Freytag's Pyramid, you can create a compelling snapshot of your story that showcases its narrative arc and emotional depth.

APPENDIX 3: THE FIRST THIRD

When writing a blurb for any book, it's essential to ensure that the first third of your story or argument is well-structured and engaging. If you're telling someone how to master a new skill, make sure they understand where they'll end up after reading your book. This is where you set expectations.

By assessing key elements of your narrative (or plan/outline) at this stage, you can create a blurb that accurately reflects the essence of your book and captivates potential readers.

Start by identifying your protagonist(s) or your reader. Typically, there is one main character or reader who should be established early on, along with their setting and period. If you're writing fiction, make sure your protagonist is active and their motivations are clear to both you and your readers. With non-fiction, consider your reader your main character. the person sitting opposite you asking for help or waiting to hear your argument.

Next, be honest about the genre of your novel or book. Whether you're writing in a specific genre like crime-thriller or science fiction, or crafting a more general story such as a love story or coming-of-age tale, a self-help tome or a guide to planting flowers, make sure that the tone (and plot elements/contents) are consistent and meet reader expectations.

By the end of the first third of your book, readers should be engaged.

In fiction, we talk about an 'inciting incident' - the point where the story starts to need to happen. This event disrupts the status quo and generates the story's momentum. Your main character should be facing challenges and conflicts, both external (such as an antagonist or opposing force) and internal (personal struggles or dilemmas). Ensure that your protagonist is in jeopardy by this point, with high stakes and much to lose. This creates tension and keeps readers invested in the story.

In non-fiction, the equivalent of the inciting incident is often a compelling hook or a thought-provoking question that draws the reader in and sets the stage for the main argument or theme of the book. While non-fiction works may not follow the same narrative structure as fiction, they still need to capture the reader's attention and provide a clear reason for them to invest their time in reading the book. The non-fiction "inciting incident" should appear early in the book, typically within the introduction or first chapter.

Finally, evaluate your narrative structure - even if you're not telling a story as such. Have you chosen the most effective viewpoint, time, and organisation for your material? The purpose of your inciting hook is to pique the reader's curiosity, challenge their assumptions, or present a problem that the book will address.

By assessing these key elements of your novel's first

third, you can craft a blurb that accurately captures the essence of your story or book, and entices readers to dive in. A well-structured opening sets the stage for a compelling blurb that will leave readers eager to experience what you have to say.